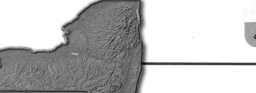

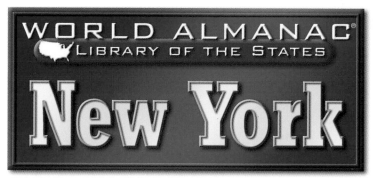

THE EMPIRE STATE

by Jackie Ball and Kristen Behrens

Curriculum Consultant: Jean Craven,
Director of Instructional Support,
Albuquerque, NM, Public Schools

WORLD ALMANAC® LIBRARY

Please visit our web site at: **www.worldalmanaclibrary.com**
**For a free color catalog describing World Almanac® Library's list of high-quality books
and multimedia programs, call 1-800-848-2928 (USA) or 1-800-387-3178 (Canada).
World Almanac® Library's fax: (414) 332-3567.**

Library of Congress Cataloging-in-Publication Data

Ball, Jacqueline A.
   New York, the Empire State / by Jackie Ball and Kristen Behrens.
     p. cm. — (World Almanac Library of the states)
   Includes bibliographical references and index.
   Summary: Illustrations and text present the history, geography, people, politics and
government, economy, and social life and customs of the Empire State.
   ISBN 0-8368-5118-8 (lib. bdg.)
   ISBN 0-8368-5288-5 (softcover)
   1. New York (State)—Juvenile literature. [1. New York (State).] I. Behrens, Kristen.
II. Title. III. Series.
F119.3.B34   2002
974.7—dc21   2001046995

This edition first published in 2002 by
World Almanac® Library
330 West Olive Street, Suite 100
Milwaukee, WI 53212 USA

This edition © 2002 by World Almanac® Library.

Design and Editorial: **Jack&Bill**/Bill SMITH STUDIO Inc.
Editors: Jackie Ball and Kristen Behrens
Art Directors: Ron Leighton and Jeffrey Rutzky
Photo Research and Buying: Christie Silver and Sean Livingstone
Design and Production: Maureen O'Connor and Jeffrey Rutzky
World Almanac® Library Editors: Patricia Lantier, Amy Stone, Valerie J. Weber,
Catherine Gardner, Carolyn Kott Washburne, Alan Wachtel, Monica Rausch
World Almanac® Library Production: Scott M. Krall, Eva Erato-Rudek, Tammy Gruenewald,
Katherine A. Goedheer

Photo credits: p. 4 © PhotoDisc; p. 6 (all) © Corel; p. 7 (clockwise) © Corel, © ArtToday,
© PhotoDisc; p. 9 © Corel; p. 10 © Bettmann/CORBIS; p. 11 © Library of Congress; p. 12
© 2001 N.Y.S. Department of Economic Development; p. 13 © Dover Publications; p. 14
© Jeffrey Rutzky; p. 17 © Bettmann/CORBIS; p. 18 © PhotoDisc; p. 19 © Corel; p. 20–23 (all)
© Corel; p. 26 (from left to right) © PhotoDisc, courtesy of NYSE; p. 27 © Corel; p. 29 © 2001
N.Y.S. Department of Economic Development; p. 30 courtesy of NY General Assembly; p. 31 (all)
Dover Publications; p. 32 © Bernard Obermann/CORBIS; p. 33 (all) © Corel; p. 34 © Corel; p. 35
© Corel; p. 36 (top) © Library of Congress, (bottom) © Library of Congress; p. 38 (from left to
right) © Dover Publications, © PhotoDisc; p. 39 © Hulton-Deutsch Collection/CORBIS; p. 40
(clockwise) © Dover Publications, © Dover Publications, © PhotoDisc; p. 41 © PhotoDisc;
p. 42–43 © Library of Congress; p. 44 (from left to right) © Jeffrey Rutzky, © Corel; p. 45 (top)
© Corel, (bottom) © PhotoDisc

All rights reserved. No part of this book may be reproduced, stored in a retrieval system,
or transmitted in any form or by any means, electronic, mechanical, photocopying, recording,
or otherwise, without the prior written permission of the copyright holder.

Printed in the United States of America

2 3 4 5 6 7 8 9 06 05 04 03

New York

Two Worlds in One

One look at the map will give you an important clue to understanding New York State — its shape. Wide and expansive at the top, it gets narrower and narrower until it drops down to the Atlantic Ocean. The striking difference between the state's shape top to bottom mirrors the dramatic differences in lifestyle, culture, geography, weather, and politics between its upper and lower reaches. In fact, New York State is so full of contradictions it's almost two different worlds.

One world is typified by New York City, the biggest city in the state — and the country. More than 40 percent of New Yorkers live in this glittering, supercharged symbol of power and prestige at the state's southern end. These eight million residents are packed into a tiny sliver that takes up less than 1 percent of the state's 47,214 square miles (122,284 square kilometers). Another 40 percent of New York's residents live in smaller cities and suburbs. The smallest percentage of the population, however, lives on the largest amount of land. Some of "upstate" New York is as sparsely populated as parts of Nevada.

New York looks something like a lopsided funnel and over time has acted as one, too. Through the gigantic inland waterway made of the Hudson and Mohawk Rivers, the St. Lawrence Seaway, and the Erie Canal have funneled countless billions of tons of lumber, steel, flour, apples, oil, and other goods from the Great Lakes to the Atlantic. The goods meant billions of dollars flowing back up into the state, giving New York a mighty position in industry and commerce worthy of its nickname, the Empire State.

Some say George Washington coined that name in 1784. Since even before then, New York has been a symbol of independence and a haven for seekers of all kinds of freedoms. In the sixteenth century Italian explorer Giovanni da Verrazano gazed on its shores and called the place "delightful and charming in appearance." Today people simply say — or sing — "I love New York."

▶ *Right:* Map of New York State, showing interstate highway system, as well as major cities and waterways.

Below right: Map of New York City, showing the five boroughs as well as New York's major airports and several important tourist sites.

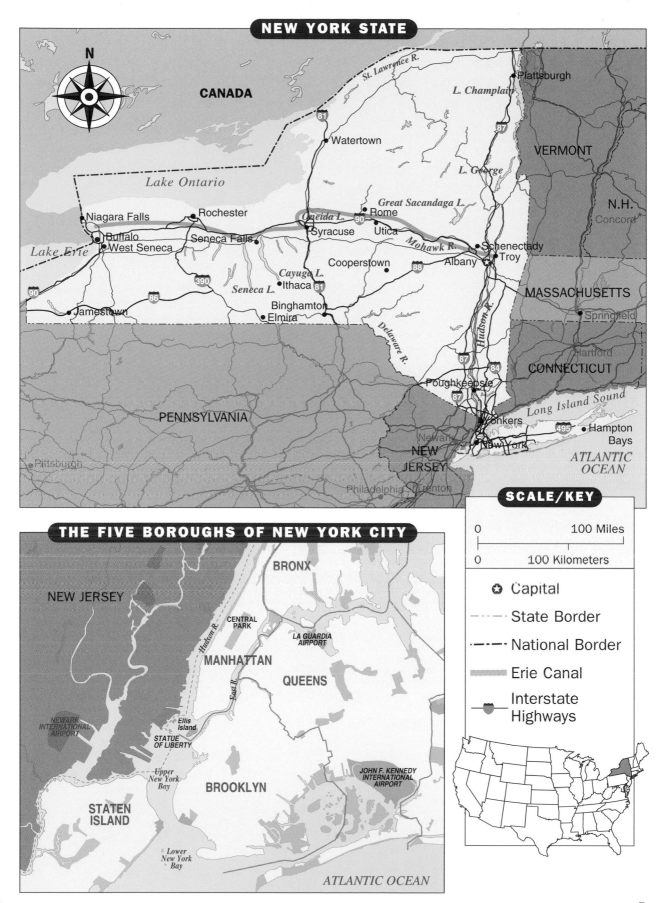

NEW YORK STATE

N

CANADA

St. Lawrence R.

Plattsburgh

L. Champlain

VERMONT

Watertown

Lake Ontario

L. George

N.H.

Concord

Great Sacandaga L.

Niagara Falls

Rochester

Oneida L.

Rome

Syracuse

Utica

Mohawk R.

Schenectady

Troy

MASSACHUSETTS

Buffalo

West Seneca

Seneca Falls

Lake Erie

Cooperstown

Albany

Springfield

Cayuga L.

Seneca L.

Ithaca

Hartford

Jamestown

Binghamton

Elmira

Delaware R.

CONNECTICUT

Hudson R.

PENNSYLVANIA

Poughkeepsie

Long Island Sound

Yonkers

Hampton Bays

Newark

NEW JERSEY

New York

ATLANTIC OCEAN

Pittsburgh

Philadelphia

Trenton

THE FIVE BOROUGHS OF NEW YORK CITY

BRONX

NEW JERSEY

CENTRAL PARK

LA GUARDIA AIRPORT

Hudson R.

MANHATTAN

QUEENS

East R.

NEWARK INTERNATIONAL AIRPORT

Ellis Island

STATUE OF LIBERTY

Upper New York Bay

JOHN F. KENNEDY INTERNATIONAL AIRPORT

BROOKLYN

STATEN ISLAND

Lower New York Bay

ATLANTIC OCEAN

SCALE/KEY

| 0 | 100 Miles |
| 0 | 100 Kilometers |

✪ Capital

State Border

National Border

Erie Canal

Interstate Highways

Fast Facts

NEW YORK (NY), The Empire State

Entered Union

July 26, 1788 (11th state)

Capital	Population
Albany	95,658

Total Population (2000)

18,976,457 (3rd most populous state)

Largest Cities	Population
New York City	8,008,278
Buffalo	292,648
Rochester	219,773
Yonkers	196,086
Syracuse	147,306

Land Area

47,214 square miles (122,284 sq km)
(30th largest state)

State Motto

"Excelsior" — *Latin for "Ever Upward"*

State Song

"I Love New York" *by Steve Karmen*

State Animal

Beaver — *Early settlers made a living selling beaver pelts to Europe.*

State Bird

Eastern Bluebird — *The population of this bird was dwindling in the 1950s. Now, as a result of public and private efforts, its numbers are on the rise again.*

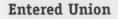

State Fish

Brook Trout — *Also known as "brookies" or "speckles."*

State Insect

Ladybug — *This member of the beetle family helps gardeners by eating insect pests.*

State Tree

Sugar Maple

State Flower

Rose — *Wild and cultivated roses, in all their variety and colors, were made the state flower in 1955. When the state flower was chosen, leaders felt that the varieties of roses reflected the diversity of the state.*

State Shell

Bay Scallop

State Gem

Wine-Red Garnet

State Beverage

Milk

State Fruit

Apple — *Early European settlers brought apple seeds with them to the region that became New York.*

State Muffin

Apple Muffin — *Centuries after the European settlers arrived, students at Bear Road Elementary School perfected a recipe for muffins using the state fruit. They also helped persuade the governor to sign a bill declaring the apple muffin the official state muffin.*

PLACES TO VISIT

National Baseball Hall of Fame, *Cooperstown*
In addition to the baseball museum, the Cooperstown area also features a farm museum and a collection of late eighteenth- and early nineteenth-century buildings. This was the hometown of novelist James Fenimore Cooper, author of *The Last of the Mohicans*.

Fort Ticonderoga on *Lake Champlain*
During the Revolutionary War Ethan Allen and his men forced the British to surrender here in 1775. The present-day fort is a reconstruction.

United Nations, *New York City*
This complex was made the world headquarters of the United Nations in 1945. It is considered an international zone and  is owned by the participating countries.

For other places and events to attend, see p. 44.

BIGGEST, BEST, AND MOST

- The Verrazano Narrows Bridge, connecting Staten Island and Brooklyn, is the longest suspension bridge in the United States.

- Alexander Graham Bell made the first transcontinental telephone call on January 25, 1915, from New York to his assistant, Watson, in San Francisco.

- More libraries can be found in New York than in any other state.

STATE FIRSTS

- 1747 — The first cattle ranch in what is now the United States was started in Montauk, New York, on the eastern tip of Long Island.

- 1831 — The first railroad in the United States ran between Albany and Schenectady, a distance of 11 miles (17.7 km).

- 1901 — New York was the first state to require license plates on cars.

Nicknaming a Nation

When Samuel Wilson of Troy, New York, received a contract to supply meat to U.S. troops during the War of 1812, he packed the meat in barrels marked "U.S." This abbreviation had not yet become common, and his workers asked what the initials stood for. As a joke, they were told it  meant Uncle Sam. Over the years Uncle Sam became a nickname for the United States, personified by the famous recruiting posters of World War I. In 1961 Congress recognized Samuel Wilson as the man behind the symbol.

Chip on His Shoulder?

When a diner at an elegant hotel in Saratoga Springs, a resort town north of Albany, complained that the french fries were too thick, the chef, George Crum, a Native American, decided to retaliate. He cut the potatoes so thin that they would be impossible to eat with a fork. The diner loved Crum's new invention, and the hotel added them to its menu, calling them Saratoga chips. Eventually, they became a New York and New England specialty, and Crum opened his own restaurant at which he featured the chips.

A Pleasant and Fruitful Country

> They goe in Deere skins loose, well dressed. They have yellow Copper. They desire Cloathes and are very civill. They have a great store of Maiz or Indian Wheate, whereof they make good Bread.
>
> — *Johannes de Laet*, Chronicles of the Hudson

Most historians believe the first humans arrived in North America around 20,000 years ago. People traveled to what would become New York State as much as eight thousand years ago. Over thousands of years several different cultures emerged.

The Algonquians occupied territory extending through the Hudson River Valley out to the Atlantic seaboard. Inland, farming the rich soil of the Mohawk River Valley, were the Iroquois. For many years the Iroquois and the Algonquians were at war. Different Iroquois tribes fought with each other, too — although many of the skirmishes were minor matters of property — until the Iroquois Confederacy was formed in about 1570 and peace came.

Together the tribes in the Confederacy called themselves "the people of the longhouse." The longhouse was the most common structure in their settlements. Each long, narrow building was able to hold many families. The longhouse, though, was more than housing; it represented the political system of the Iroquois. Historians compare the confederacy to a giant longhouse, stretching across upstate New York, its chiefs like posts that supported the society.

Although at that time war was a fact of life, so was a tradition of equality and community. Some historians argue that the Iroquois society was a model for the government of the United States, with equal rights and inherent respect for the individual.

Algonquian Member Nations
Montauk
Munsee
Delaware
Wappinger
Mahican (Mohegan)

Iroquois Member Nations (Also known as the Five Nations)
Cayuga
Mohawk
Oneida
Onondaga
Seneca

The Coming of the Europeans

Some believed it to be an uncommonly large fish or animal, while others thought it was a very big house floating on the sea.

— Native Americans' reported reactions to first sight of Henry Hudson's ship, the *Half Moon*

The first European to visit New York was probably Giovanni da Verrazano, an Italian who had been sent to explore the area by the French in 1524. He visited present-day New York Harbor.

▼ The Hudson River, pictured below as it looked in the 1800s, has been vital to New York's economy since the days of the earliest settlers.

▲ An artist's rendition
of Henry Hudson
coming ashore in
New York.

In 1609 Frenchman Samuel de Champlain traveled south from Canada to northern New York. Lake Champlain is named after him. Also in 1609 Englishman Henry Hudson, working for a Dutch company, sailed about 100 miles (161 km) up what is now the Hudson River, looking for a route to the Pacific Ocean. Hudson did not find it, but he claimed the area for the Dutch and called it New Netherland.

In 1624 Dutch settlers built Fort Orange near where New York's capital, Albany, is today. In 1625 another settlement was founded, this one located at one end of a small island at the mouth of the Hudson. Dutch governor Peter Minuit supposedly paid the Algonquians, its Native residents, beads and trinkets worth 60 guilders, or about $24, for the island they called *Mana-Hatta* (Manhattan). Minuit named the settlement New Amsterdam.

For forty years more Dutch settlers came to live along the Hudson. They farmed and traded with the Indians for beaver and otter pelts. Meanwhile, to the south, New Amsterdam was filling up with people from all over Europe — the kind of rich ethnic mix that would become New York City's trademark.

New Amsterdam's population grew, and so did its influence on trade. Most ships carrying cargo in and out of the colonies had to pass through New York Harbor. England, already in control of all the other colonies along the Atlantic, wanted New Amsterdam, too, and in 1664 sent warships. Dutch governor Peter Stuyvesant surrendered. Five years later New Amsterdam was renamed New York after the English Duke of York.

The French and Indian War (1754–1763)

The Dutch no longer stood in the way of total British dominance in the Atlantic colonies, but there were the French to worry about. Britain and France both wanted to control the profitable Indian fur trade. The French and Indian War broke out after France started building forts from the St. Lawrence River, in Canada, south to the Mississippi River, in territory claimed by the English colony of Virginia. Both sides employed the Indians: The Iroquois sided with the British; the Algonquians allied themselves with the French.

Early on, the British army suffered many defeats, including the loss of Fort Oswego on the Canadian border. This left settlers there open to Indian and French attack. In 1758, however, England sent better-trained soldiers. By 1759 Quebec was captured, France was soon defeated, and the war ended in 1763 with the Treaty of Paris.

New Nation

The exposing therefore of Publick (sic) Wickedness, as it is a Duty which every Man owes to the Truth and his Country, can never be a Libel in the Nature of Things
— From the libel trial of John Peter Zenger

With the peace came thousands more settlers. Now, however, new tensions filled the air. Groups of colonists who called themselves Patriots were becoming impatient with British rule. At the same time colonists called Loyalists were faithful to England.

The *New-York Weekly Journal*

This political paper, published by John Peter Zenger (1697–1746), contained articles attacking the colony's unpopular royal governor, William Cosby, calling him an "idiot" and a "rogue." As a result, Zenger was arrested for libel in 1734, which at that time meant the publication of a damaging statement about someone — whether or not it was true.

The jury, in spite of instructions from the judge that truth was not a defense against libel, found that the statements in the newspaper were true and that Zenger was not guilty. A pioneer in journalism, Zenger paved the way for the establishment of freedom of the press in the American colonies.

◄ A reenactment of the Battle of Saratoga in 1777, a British defeat that marked a turning point in the Revolutionary War.

In April 1775 the first shots of the Revolutionary War were fired in Massachusetts. On July 9, 1776, New York authorized its delegates to the Continental Congress to approve the Declaration of Independence, which had been adopted on July 4. At the same time New York's own state government was set up. Three days later British warships sailed into New York Harbor and the battles began. Eventually ninety-two Revolutionary War battles would be fought in the state. Finally, on November 25, 1783, British troops left New York City, which they had occupied for most of the war. A new, free nation was born.

Sadly, however, it *wasn't* an entirely free nation — or state. Slavery was still accepted practice in the North and the South. In New York the Iroquois suffered terrible and lasting losses. Retaliating for Iroquois support of the British, General George Washington had ordered an all-out attack on Iroquois settlements in the Finger Lakes region in 1777. The Iroquois confederacy was shattered, and the "longhouse" smashed into splinters.

Further settlement occurred after the War of 1812 with England, when soldiers were given land grants. By 1820 New York was home to over 1,370,000 people — more than any other state in the Union. The state was growing fast, so what could be more fitting than a fast new means of transportation?

A Shameful Past

In 1626 Dutch settlers brought eleven African slaves to New York City. By 1740 slaves made up 21 percent of the city's population.

In 1799 the New York State legislature first took steps to abolish slavery, declaring that children born to slaves would be free as of age twenty-eight for men and twenty-four for women. Finally, in 1817, July 4, 1827, was picked as the day when all slaves within the state of New York would be free.

Full Steam Ahead

Scientists and inventors had been working on a steam-powered boat since 1630, when an English patent had been granted to David Ramseye "to make shippes and barges goe against strong wind and tide." However, it was New Yorker Robert Fulton who got the financial backing to make a working steam engine a reality. In 1809 Fulton traveled up the Hudson on his 130-foot (40-meter), paddle-wheeled North River Steamboat, later called the *Clermont*.

East Meets West

The coming of the steamship revolutionized passenger travel. At the same time New York's economic and political leaders were trying to figure out how to ship goods across the state and to other states — even to Europe. One big idea: dig a long trench, a canal, connecting Lake Erie to the Hudson River. Although many jeered at the idea — even Thomas Jefferson called it "madness" — the Erie Canal was completed in 1825. It crossed the state from Buffalo on Lake Erie to Troy and Albany on the Hudson. The canal became an important link in an all-water route between New York City and Buffalo.

On a Fast Track

Now the state had an inland water-highway connecting its interior portions and leading to the sea. Soon there was an overland system, too. In 1831 New York's first railroad, the Mohawk and Hudson, began running between Albany and Schenectady. It was followed by Cornelius Vanderbilt's New York Central. Eventually the railroad was extended to New York City. Construction of the canal and the railroad provided jobs for many of the thousands of European immigrants pouring into the state. By 1850 New York was indeed an "empire:" a leader, number one in the nation in population, manufacturing, and commerce.

The state was also about to become a leader in a new political movement: reform. New Yorkers were angry about unfair practices and wanted action.

Reform Movement

The earliest protest came in 1839, when tenant farmers refused to pay rent to wealthy landlords. They eventually won the right to own the land themselves. In 1848

**Robert Fulton
(1765–1815)
Designer of the First
Working Steamboat**

The first steamboats were noisy and sent off a brilliant "galaxy of sparks." Crews of nearby ships were awestruck, as this account indicates: "When the steamboat came so near that the noise of the machinery and paddles were heard, the crews in some instances shrunk beneath the decks from the terrific sight, and left their vessels to go on shore, while others prostrated themselves and besought Providence to protect them from the approach of the horrible monster which was marching on the tides and lighting up its path by the fires which it vomited."

Elizabeth Cady Stanton and Lucretia Mott held the first major women's rights conference, at Seneca Falls, producing a Declaration of Sentiments that argued for women's right to the vote.

Meanwhile, new manufacturing centers drew new waves of job-seeking immigrants to New York City. By 1900 more than 25 percent of the state's population was made up of people who had entered the country by way of Ellis Island in New York Harbor. The Statue of Liberty has stood as a symbol of freedom in the harbor since 1886.

Twentieth Century

All eyes were on New York State in 1901. In September President William McKinley was fatally shot by an anarchist at the Pan-American exposition in Buffalo. Vice President Theodore Roosevelt, former governor of New York, became president.

New York City was a financial hub. Bankers and industrialists prospered, but for workers, conditions and wages were usually poor. In 1911 a fire at the Triangle Shirtwaist Company in New York City killed 146 people, mostly women and girls, who had been locked into the building to keep them at their posts. This disaster resulted in workplace safety laws and restrictions on child labor and also triggered a new interest in labor unions, especially among immigrant workers.

The United States entered World War I in 1917. Thousands of U.S. troops left for Europe through the port of New York. When the war ended in 1918, they returned

Declaration of Sentiments

We hold these truths to be self-evident: that all men and women are created equal; that they are endowed by their Creator with certain inalienable rights; that among these are life, liberty, and the pursuit of happiness; that to secure these rights governments are instituted, deriving their just powers from the consent of the governed.

Whenever any form of government becomes destructive of these ends, it is the right of those who suffer from it to refuse allegiance to it . . .

Elizabeth Cady Stanton, Declaration of Sentiments

▼ **The Manhattan skyline.**

home through that same port, where the economy was booming. A decade later, however, the New York City-based stock market collapsed (in October of 1929), triggering the Great Depression. Millions were jobless. In 1932 New York Governor Franklin D. Roosevelt was elected president, promising programs to help out-of-work Americans based on those he had started in New York.

War and Peace

The United States entered World War II in 1941. New York was the point of departure for half the nation's Europe-bound forces. The whole state was involved in producing arms, uniforms, vehicles, and other military materials.

After the war ended the United Nations was formed, and in 1950 construction on its home in New York City was begun. All around the state, bridges, highways, and waterways were constructed, including the St. Lawrence Seaway, which allowed large ocean-going ships to travel between the Atlantic and the Great Lakes.

The 1970s saw factory closings and loss of jobs, but by the middle of the decade, the economy was recovering and, with a few bumps, has continued to improve. Today the poor still face problems finding housing and social services. The state must also find funds to improve transportation and education.

In spite of these issues, immigrants from many places keep pouring into New York City. This continually changing ethnic and racial mix keeps the tip of the "funnel" among the most diverse populations in the country and gives the

state a position second only to California in the number of immigrants it receives each year.

New York's strength and spirit were never tested as greatly, or made more apparent, as in the aftermath of a terrorist attack on September 11, 2001, that devastated the World Trade Center in New York City. In the weeks following the attack, New Yorkers pulled together in support of each other as well as police, firefighters, and rescue and recovery workers.

Centuries of New Beginnings

> . . . remarkable and ever-recurring revolutions
> in ethnic make-up.
> — *Theodore Roosevelt,* An Autobiography, *1913*

Teddy Roosevelt's description is just as true of today's New York City — and New York State — as it was more than a century ago. There are millions of New Yorkers — 18,976,457 as of the year 2000 to be exact. Many either were not born in the United States or are the children of immigrant parents. In the state as a whole, this is true of about 20 percent of the population. In New York City, where almost half the state's population lives, the percentage is much higher. And this is not a new phenomenon. In 1860 nearly half of New York City's residents were foreign-born.

For many years New York Harbor has been the entry point for new citizens from all over the world. In the late 1800s and early 1900s, as many as five thousand immigrants a day, many of them from southern and eastern Europe, were processed by U.S. immigration officials on Ellis Island. A hundred years later a higher proportion of immigrants are from Asia and Latin America.

DID YOU KNOW?

The population of New York City is the highest of any city in the United States. In fact it has a higher population than thirty-nine of the fifty states.

Homelands of Largest Foreign-Born Groups in NYC

	1890				1990				
Austria	Russia	England	Ireland	Germany	China	India	Russia	Italy	Central American
28,626	52,187	62,400	275,156	305,521	42,286	42,367	79,701	96,339	162,682

◀ More than 1.5 million people came to the U.S. from Ireland alone. Most of them, like the family on the left, arrived in New York City, where many stayed. After a difficult ocean crossing, they often found work as servants and doing construction work. Eventually, they built churches, developed a system of church-related schools, worked to form labor unions, and became an important political force.

A Better Life

Regardless of the immigrants' countries of origin, the result is the same today as it was then: a diverse population, influenced by an ever-increasing number of cultures. The reasons for immigration are also the same: to live under better economic conditions and to escape from religious or political persecution. New York's attitude of tolerance toward religious groups and many nationalities dates back to the earliest days of Dutch-controlled New Amsterdam, which welcomed religious minorities such as Quakers and Jews as well as immigrants from all over Europe. Even as early as the 1640s, it is said that fifteen different languages were spoken in the city.

Age Distribution in New York

0–4	1,239,417
5–19	3,971,834
20–24	1,244,309
25–44	5,831,622
45–64	4,240,923
65 and over	2,448,352

Heritage and Background, New York State — Year 2000

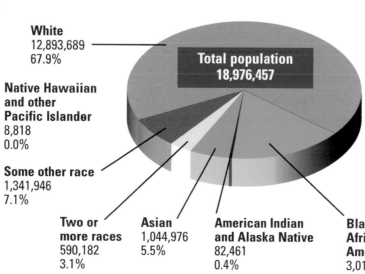

▶ Here's a look at the racial backgrounds of New Yorkers today. New York ranks eleventh in the country with regard to African Americans as a percentage of the population.

Total population 18,976,457

White 12,893,689 67.9%

Native Hawaiian and other Pacific Islander 8,818 0.0%

Some other race 1,341,946 7.1%

Two or more races 590,182 3.1%

Asian 1,044,976 5.5%

American Indian and Alaska Native 82,461 0.4%

Black or African American 3,014,385 15.9%

Note: 15.1% (2,867,583) of the population identify themselves as **Hispanic** or **Latino,** a cultural designation that crosses racial lines. Hispanics and Latinos are counted in this category and the racial category of their choice.

Where Do New Yorkers Live?

Most of the more than eighteen million New Yorkers live in cities, suburbs, and towns. More than 2.25 million live in Westchester and Nassau Counties, within easy commuting distance of New York City. At the other end of the state, the Buffalo metropolitan area is home to almost 1.2 million people. Small towns, farms, and rural areas are still home to many New Yorkers.

Education

Overall, the population of New York today is well educated. The great majority of the work force has at least completed high school, and a higher percentage of New York workers

Educational Levels of New York Workers	
Less than 9th grade	372,308
9th to 12th grade, no diploma	902,759
High school graduate, including equivalency	2,399,362
Some college, no degree or associate degree	2,355,304
Bachelor's degree	1,388,034
Graduate or professional degree	974,074

Ellis Island

Ellis Island opened in 1892. Its job was to process steerage passengers — those traveling in the cramped, dark quarters below deck, described by English writer Charles Dickens as "a little world of poverty."

At Ellis Island passengers were checked for diseases, criminal records, and more. Over twelve million people passed through the processing center before it closed in 1954.

▼ Ellis Island today. It is now a museum visited by millions of tourists annually.

have attended college than in the nation as a whole.

New York is a relatively old state, with a median age of 35.9 years, nearly a year older than the national average. Compare that to other highly populated states like California and Texas, where it's 33.3 and 32.3, respectively.

The enormous wave of eastern and southern European immigrants in the late 1800s and early 1900s, many of whom were either Roman Catholic or Jewish, played a large part in establishing New York's two leading religious affiliations. African-American groups have also had an impact: New York is the state with the eleventh-highest population of African Americans.

▲ Among New York City cabdrivers, as many as sixty different languages are spoken.

Religion

New Yorkers practice many different religions. About 40 percent of New Yorkers are Catholic, and nearly 10 percent are Jewish. Among the many different Protestant Christian groups that New Yorkers belong to are Baptist, Methodist, Episcopalian, Presbyterian, and Lutheran churches. Muslims make up about 0.8 percent of the New York population, and 0.2 percent of the population are practicing Buddhists. About 0.6 percent of the New York State population are Hindu, and about the same percent are agnostic — neither believing nor disbelieving in God.

Old + New = Tension

New York's extraordinary diversity has made for some tense times. Historically, newly arrived populations do not always blend in easily with the more established groups. The older groups feel threatened by a new labor force whose customs they may view as strange. The newer groups often feel exploited by poor working conditions and prejudicial treatment. Still, it seems likely that the "ever-recurring revolutions in ethnic make-up" will continue into the twenty-first century, not only in New York City but in the whole state. New immigrants will bring new skills and traditions, which, like others before them, will be incorporated into the daily work and cultural life of all the state's residents.

A Rich and Rugged Landscape

> Nature has been very lavish here in the gifts of her beauty.
> — *Frederic Edwin Church, painter, in a letter to Henry Wadsworth Longfellow*

New York's landscape is as diverse as its population. The state is a patchwork of farmland and forests, with ancient mountains, important rivers, and glistening ocean beaches. With that variety in its physical features comes dramatic differences in weather and wildlife.

DID YOU KNOW?

The New York cities of Syracuse, Rochester, and Buffalo receive a greater annual snowfall than any other large cities in the nation.

Climate

New York tends to have wet springs, warm summers, and cool falls. Temperatures between the far north and the far south of the state, however, can vary by as much as 15° Fahrenheit (8.4° Celsius) in summer and 20°F (11.2°C) or more in winter. The south tends to get far less snowfall in winter; its proximity to the ocean also ensures that the snow doesn't stick. New York City, and especially Long Island, are also buffeted by hurricanes that make their way up the coast from Florida in the fall.

Coastlines, Beaches, Harbors, Sounds, Islands

Although the vast majority of New York State is landlocked, the southernmost tip contains important harbors and coastline. It was this access to the Atlantic Ocean that allowed New York to establish itself initially as a major merchant city and later as a major industrial center. New

▼ *From left to right:* **A Montauk lighthouse; a coyote; Niagara Falls; an upstate vineyard; Central Park in New York City; B & B Buffalo Ranch in Ellicotville.**

York Harbor, at the mouth of the Hudson, is a deep natural harbor almost completely protected by land.

New York's three largest islands, Long Island, Manhattan Island, and Staten Island, all have access to both the Atlantic Ocean and the Hudson River, allowing them to grow as both centers of industry and thriving ports. All three islands are densely populated.

New York's borders are partially created by two of the five Great Lakes. That, plus access to the St. Lawrence Seaway, means that goods can cross the state and move farther west into the United States. In addition goods can come down from Canada on into New York and beyond.

New York State contains more than eight thousand lakes, providing the state with great natural beauty as well as resources for both fishing and water consumption. In addition the Finger Lakes, naturally existing bodies of water in the middle of the state, helped ease the problems of constructing the Erie Canal. Lake Champlain also connects to the St. Lawrence Seaway.

Major Rivers

The Delaware, Hudson, and Mohawk Rivers allow for transporting goods into the interior of the state. The Hudson River has been the most important, especially since the opening of the Erie Canal.

Mountains

New York's mountains, while not very high compared to those in the western United States, are among the oldest in the world. The heavily wooded regions were very important to the lumber industry.

Flora and Fauna

The variety of types of habitats in New York State means an enormous biological diversity. The state is heavily populated:

Average January temperature
New York City: 32°F (0°C)
Buffalo: 24°F (-4°C)

Average July temperature
New York City: 77°F (25°C)
Buffalo: 71°F (21°C)

Average yearly rainfall
New York City: 47.2 inches (120 centimeters)
Buffalo: 35.6 inches (90.4 cm)

Average yearly snowfall
New York City: 29.2 inches (74 cm)
Buffalo: 82.5 inches (209 cm)

Major Rivers

Delaware River
405 miles (650 km) total, 325 miles (523 km) within New York State

Hudson River
308 miles (494 km)

Mohawk River
140 miles (225 km)

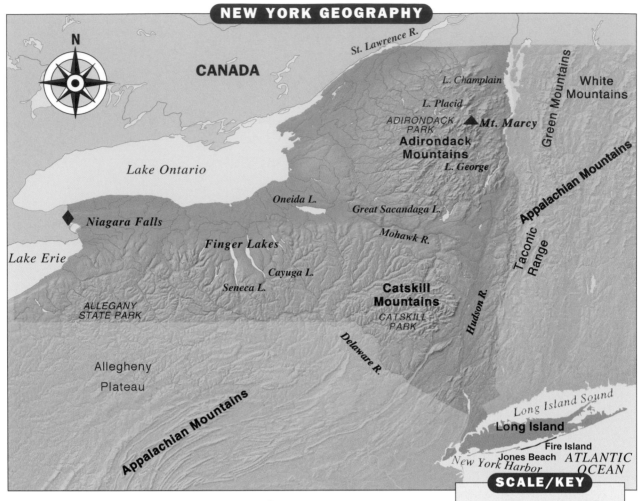

SCALE/KEY

| 0 | 100 Miles |
| 0 | 100 Kilometers |

◆ Landmark
▲ Highest Point
▨ Mountains

328 species of birds, 93 species of mammals, 490 marine and freshwater fish species, and 73 species of reptiles and amphibians call New York home. Some animals are as common as the beach roses dotting the sand dunes at Montauk, the state's easternmost point, or as the sugar maples and evergreens covering the millions of acres of forest and mountains. Others, however, are as unusual as the silver chub and the Allegheny woodrat, both endangered species. Wildlife sanctuaries in Dutchess and Columbia Counties provide nesting places for thousands of great blue herons, hummingbirds, and red-winged blackbirds.

New York's periods of economic growth have resulted in increased development, which in turn has threatened certain animal habitats. Deer and coyote are now roaming farther into suburbs and cities. Now New York is seeking to safeguard its wildlife with legislation and by working with agencies such as the National Audubon Society.

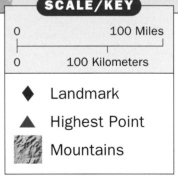

High Points

Adirondack Mountains
Mt. Marcy
5,344 feet (1,629 m)

Catskill Mountains
Mt. Slide
4,206 feet (1,282 m)

Environment

Although New York State contains the largest semi-wilderness area east of the Mississippi — 18 million acres (7,284,600 hectares) in Adirondack State Park — it is also the state with the third-highest population nationwide. Many more people commute to and from New York from nearby areas each day. The number of people puts a heavy toll on the state's environment.

For instance, New York City's large population produces a lot of sewage, some of which makes it into the surrounding waters. Although the state has undertaken a recycling program, it still must dispose of more than four million tons of solid waste each year. Most of the garbage is disposed of in landfills. Unfortunately harmful materials from the landfill can seep into soil and water. New York is trying to close its landfills, but it has not yet found an alternative disposal method.

All those people means lots of cars. The U.S. Environmental Protection Agency estimates that air toxins from motor vehicles may cause as many as fifteen hundred cases of cancer in the country each year. Car emissions also contribute to acid rain and global warming and are the single largest contributor to ground level ozone, a major component of smog. Ozone causes problems such as coughing and wheezing and can cause permanent lung damage. Cars also emit several pollutants classified as air toxins, which can adversely affect the human respiratory and nervous systems.

Finally, New York is home to many industries, some of which produce toxic chemicals, heavy metals such as lead and mercury, and other hazardous compounds. These, too, can create enormous health hazards; in the 1970s, PCB (polychlorinated biphenyl), a toxic chemical, contaminated the water and soil of a suburban community near Niagara Falls called Love Canal.

▶ Coyotes, native to the state, have re-established their population in New York's Adirondack Park.

Largest Lakes

Lake Erie
241 miles (388 km) long
Width at widest point:
57 miles (92 km)
Size: 9,940 square miles (25,745 sq km)

Lake Ontario
193 miles (311 km) long
Width at widest point:
53 miles (85 km)
Size: 7,540 square miles (19,529 sq km)

Lake Champlain
125 miles (201 km) long
Width at widest point:
14 miles (23 km)
Size: 490 square miles (1,269 sq km)

Lake George
33 miles (53 km) long
Width at widest point:
3 miles (5 km)
Size: 25 square miles (65 sq km)

From Livestock to Stock Market

> From Long Island to the Adirondacks to my old neighborhood in the Bronx, we New Yorkers have a rich tradition of working people who have joined together.
>
> — *John J. Sweeney, AFL-CIO president*

New York's labor force is made up of about nine million people, which includes an increasing number of African Americans and Hispanics. A majority work in service industries or in wholesale or retail businesses. New York City is also a media and entertainment center; major television networks, music studios, and publishing companies are heaquartered there.

Although manufacturing is declining, the industry is still an important source of jobs, particularly in the Rochester area. Here cameras, film, copying equipment, and scientific instruments are manufactured. For many farming is a livelihood. New York ranks high among the states in dairy production.

New York's work force is very productive. More goods and services are produced by each worker than in most other places in the country. One reason for this is the high level of education in the workforce.

Twenty-five percent of New York workers belong to labor unions — the largest of any state — reflecting the significance of manufacturing to the economy, as well as the state's reform tradition.

The foundation of the state's economy is continually changing, however. Manufacturing does not play as great a role today as it did in the early and middle twentieth century. Insurance, real estate, and banking and finance have become much more important in terms of the value of goods and services produced by the state. In fact, they account for about one-third of the value of all New York's goods and services (known as the gross state product).

DID YOU KNOW?

About one-sixth of all reading materials produced in the United States are printed or published in New York City.

Top Employers
(of workers age sixteen and over; totals add up to more than 100% as some residents may hold two or more jobs)

Service industries (dry cleaners, restaurants)	37%
Wholesale or retail trade	19%
Federal, state, and local government (including military)	17%
Manufacturing	14%
Finance, insurance, and real estate	9%
Transportation and public utilities	7%
Construction	5%
Farming, fishing, and forestry	1%
Mining	1%

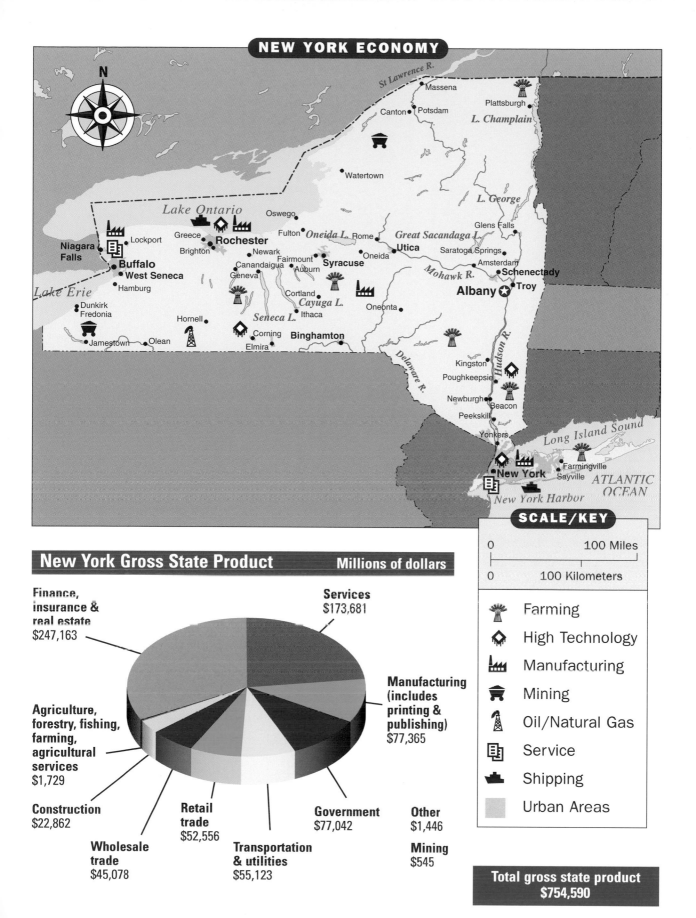

N

St Lawrence R.
Massena
Plattsburgh
Canton · Potsdam
L. Champlain

Watertown

L. George

Lake Ontario
Oswego
Glens Falls
Greece · Rochester
Fulton · Oneida L. Rome
Great Sacandaga L.
Niagara Falls
Lockport
Brighton
Newark
Utica
Saratoga Springs
Buffalo
Fairmount
Canandaigua
Syracuse
Oneida
Amsterdam
West Seneca
Geneva · Auburn
Mohawk R.
Schenectady
Hamburg
Cortland
Cayuga L.
Albany · Troy
Lake Erie
Dunkirk
Fredonia
Hornell
Seneca L. Ithaca
Oneonta
Jamestown · Olean
Corning
Binghamton
Elmira
Delaware R.
Kingston
Poughkeepsie
Hudson R.
Newburgh
Beacon
Peekskill
Yonkers
Long Island Sound
New York
Farmingville
Sayville
ATLANTIC OCEAN
New York Harbor

SCALE/KEY

0 — 100 Miles
0 — 100 Kilometers

🌾 Farming
◈ High Technology
🏭 Manufacturing
⛏ Mining
🛢 Oil/Natural Gas
🏢 Service
🚢 Shipping
▨ Urban Areas

New York Gross State Product — Millions of dollars

Finance, insurance & real estate
$247,163

Services
$173,681

Manufacturing (includes printing & publishing)
$77,365

Agriculture, forestry, fishing, farming, agricultural services
$1,729

Construction
$22,862

Retail trade
$52,556

Government
$77,042

Other
$1,446

Wholesale trade
$45,078

Transportation & utilities
$55,123

Mining
$545

**Total gross state product
$754,590**

High Finance

New York State's first commercial bank, the Bank of New York, opened in New York City in 1784. By 1791 it had an office on the corner of Wall and William Streets, near the Wall Street office of the First Bank of the United States. Since then the term *Wall Street* has come to mean a powerful international center of high finance. Even the disruption caused by the World Trade Center calamity on September 11, 2001, didn't slow Wall Street down for long.

The bustling, high-tech New York Stock Exchange (NYSE), in the heart of New York City's financial district, is the largest marketplace in the world for trading securities (stocks and bonds). Nearby, the American Stock Exchange has its headquarters. Brokerage houses, law firms, insurance companies, and other businesses related to the stock exchanges are found in the surrounding areas.

Where Apples Are *Really* Big

New York City may be the center for high finance, but when it comes to agriculture, upstate New York is the Big Apple. Or rather, it's big *in* apples — they're New York's major

▲ Wall Street, New York City — one of the financial capitals of the world.

Made in New York

Leading farm products and crops
Milk and dairy
   products
Apples
Cherries
Grapes
Corn
Hay
Alfalfa

Other products
Printed materials
Scientific
   instruments
Crushed stone
Machinery

fruit, growing in several thousand orchards. Grapes for wine are grown in the Catskills, Long Island, and the western part of the state. New York is also one of the top producers of dairy products in the country, with more than ten thousand dairy farms churning out more than 80 million gallons (304 million liters) of milk every month. Other farms raise beef cattle, pigs, ducks, and crops.

Geography is a big reason behind New York's agricultural success. Plants grow particularly well because of the mineral-rich soil in upstate New York's river valleys, deposited by glaciers thousands of years ago.

Planes, Trains, and Automobiles

New York State has many commercial and commuter railroads. Of the commuter railroads, the Long Island Railroad and the Metro-North Railroad are the first- and second-busiest commuter railroads in the country. The Long Island Railroad has over 701 miles (1,128 km) of track and Metro-North 775 miles (1,247 km). Amtrak also runs passenger lines throughout the state.

New York City's subway system, the busiest in the nation, services an average of 4.3 million customers per weekday and 1.3 billion passengers a year. People make their way to and from New York City not just by subway, but by helicopters and water shuttles. Nineteen million passengers ride the Staten Island Ferry each year, and other ferries travel over the Hudson River from New Jersey.

Hundreds of millions of passengers use New York's six major airports (counting Newark International in New Jersey). About 230 million vehicles a year use the thruway system. More than 640 miles (1,032 km) of the Governor Thomas E. Dewey Thruway connect New York City and Buffalo via the largest toll super-highway system in the nation. The thruway system also connects New York with neighboring Canada, Connecticut, New Jersey, Massachusetts, and Pennsylvania.

▲ There are more than 7.4 million apple trees in New York State, and in the fall of 2000, New York growers harvested more than 25 million bushels of apples. There are more than 650 orchards in the state, on approximately 55,000 acres (22,257 ha).

Major Airports		
Airport	**Location**	**Passengers per year (approx.)**
John F. Kennedy	Queens (NYC)	332,779,428
LaGuardia	Queens (NYC)	25,233,889
Buffalo-Niagara	Buffalo	4,250,474
Albany International	Albany	2,876,817
Syracuse Hancock International	Syracuse	2,137,953

A Step Ahead

> So great was George Clinton's popularity that at the first election under the new constitution he was elected both Governor and Lt. Governor. He declined the latter . . .
>
> — *Andrew McCord, 1777*

Making a State

New York ratified the U.S. Constitution on July 26, 1788, but New York had already had its own constitution for ten years. The first governor of New York, George Clinton, was elected to the office in 1777, while the Revolutionary War was still underway. New York, technically still a British colony, held a state convention and created a state constitution. It declared that the governor should be elected by the people.

The constitution also guaranteed that the citizens of New York would have the right to amend, or change, it. To this day, New Yorkers vote on whether to hold another convention to amend their constitution every twenty years. New constitutions were adopted in 1821, 1846, and 1894. The 1894 constitution has been amended more than two hundred times.

Political History

New York's political history has often been shaped by two conflicting points of view. On one side have been those fighting for increased trade and commerce and on the other those who were more insular. This has been true since the anti-Federalists, many of them wealthy landowners, opposed the building of the Erie Canal. Meanwhile, the Federalists tended to look forward to the added trade that they believed the waterway would bring to the state.

Throughout New York's history the tension over trade has remained fairly constant. As the Civil War loomed, the New York Republican Party favored fighting to preserve the Union and to abolish slavery. The Democratic Party, primarily

New York State Constitution

Resolved, That it be recommended to the respective assemblies and conventions of the United colonies, where no government sufficient to the exigencies of their affairs has been hitherto established, to adopt such government as shall, in the opinion of the representatives of the people, best conduce to the happiness and safety of their constituents in particular, and America in general.

April 20, 1777

Elected Posts in the Executive Branch		
Office	Length of Term	Term Limits
Governor	4 years	None
Lieutenant Governor	4 years	None
Attorney General	4 years	None
Secretary of State	4 years	None
State Comptroller	4 years	None

DID YOU KNOW?

On January 7, 1861, Fernando Wood, New York City's mayor, proposed that New York City declare itself independent of the Union so that the city would not be caught in a bad situation when the United States "disintegrated."

Former Vice President Aaron Burr and former Secretary of the Treasury Alexander Hamilton were bitter political enemies. They had a famous duel on July 11, 1804, and Hamilton died of his wounds. They weren't the only New Yorkers to fight duels, however. DeWitt Clinton, another opponent of Burr's, fought a duel with John Swarthout, one of Burr's supporters. Clinton escaped without injury; Swarthout was shot in the leg.

composed of politicians from New York City and the other major industrial centers, felt that their trading relationship with the South needed to be preserved and opposed the war. Eventually New York State fell in with the rest of the northern states, and at the first battle of the Civil War, Bull Run, over one-third of the casualties were New Yorkers.

As immigration spurred New York City's growth over the course of the late 1800s and early 1900s, the divide between the city and its beliefs and those of the state's more rural areas was only confirmed. Overall, a strong tradition of reform and progressive political attitudes prevailed. The state has a long liberal record on abolition, suffrage, workers' rights, and other socially progressive issues.

Executive Branch
New York holds its elections every year on the first Tuesday in November. Every four years, New Yorkers vote for the governor, who assumes office on the first of January of the following year.

The governor is responsible for appointing people to many offices. He does not, however, appoint the members of the Board of Regents, which oversees education. That board is appointed by the legislature.

◀ New York State's Capitol Building. It took thirty-two years (1867–1899) to complete.

The Legislature
Like the U.S. Congress, New York State's legislature is bicameral — composed of two houses. In New York the two houses are the state

senate and the state assembly. The state is divided into sixty-one districts, and each elects a senator. The number of assembly members each district elects depends upon the population of that district.

Legislators begin sessions on the Wednesday after the first Monday in January in the state capital, Albany. The legislature is responsible for making laws and levying taxes.

The Judicial System

In most states, as in the federal government, the highest court is the supreme court. In New York, however, the highest court is the court of appeals. It is composed of a chief judge and six associate judges. They, like all judges at the state level, serve for fourteen-year terms. The court of appeals can decide to hear appeals from cases judged by the appellate court.

Below the court of appeals are the appellate courts, which are divided into four divisions. Each handles cases from a specific region of the state. The appellate courts can decide to hear appeals from cases judged by the supreme court.

Below the appellate courts is the supreme court. There are approximately 314 supreme court judges, all of whom are elected. Sometimes a court of appeals or appellate court position needs to be filled. When that happens, the governor chooses from among the supreme court judges and the legislature approves them.

The last state court is the court of claims. It was created in 1939 and handles lawsuits against the state and its agencies. The governor nominates practicing lawyers to this court, and the state senate confirms them. The judges serve for nine-year terms and may serve for more than one term. By law, however, they must retire at age seventy.

At the local level each county has its own courts. The county courts hear civil and criminal cases that occur within that county. Within counties there are also family, town, city, and village courts.

▲ Approximately two thousand bills and resolutions are voted on annually in the Assembly Chamber. Today the votes are cast and tallied electronically.

New York State Legislature			
House	Number of Members	Length of Term	Term Limits
Senate	61 senators	2 years	None
Assembly	150 representatives	2 years	None

The White House via New York

Six New Yorkers have served as president of the United States.

MARTIN VAN BUREN (1837–1841) Soon after winning the election, the nation turned against him. The panic of 1837 was followed by a depression, and Van Buren failed to respond.

MILLARD FILLMORE (1850–1853) He supported the Compromise of 1850, establishing a Fugitive Slave Law, which guaranteed that runaway slaves would be returned to their owners.

CHESTER ALAN ARTHUR (1881–1885) A lawyer in New York City, his presidency was marked by the organization of the Alaska Territory.

GROVER CLEVELAND (1885–1889 and 1893–1897) Born in New Jersey, he was the only president to be elected to two nonconsecutive terms. Cleveland was also the only president to be married in the White House.

THEODORE ROOSEVELT (1901–1909) During his time in the White House, he designated 150 national forests, the first 51 Federal Bird Reservations, 5 national parks, the first 18 national monuments, and the first 4 national game preserves. Over seven years he provided federal protection for almost 230 million acres (93 million ha).

FRANKLIN DELANO ROOSEVELT (1933–1945) FDR was the only president to serve four consecutive terms. His time in office was marked by sweeping social programs (the New Deal) and World War II.

Local Government

New York State is divided into 62 counties, 62 cities, 932 towns, and 553 villages. Each county is generally run by a board of supervisors, which is responsible for parks, libraries, county courts, social services, and highways.

Within each county are cities, towns, and villages. Cities and towns are usually governed by a mayor and a council or a supervisor and a board of supervisors. Within a larger city or town, there may be several villages. A village often has a mayor, too. Taxes can be levied by all levels of government — state, town or city, and village. Local governments receive a share of the money state taxes raise. More than half the state's budget goes to the local governments. Local officials tend to spend most of this money on the public school system. Other funds go to highways, public housing, and welfare.

DID YOU KNOW?

The five counties that make up the city of New York are also called boroughs, and they function both as independent counties and parts of one large city.

New York State of Mind

> **Come and meet
> Those dancing feet
> On the avenue I'm taking you to
> Forty-second street**
>
> *— 42nd Street, a musical
> (lyrics by Al Dubin, music by Harry Warren)*

DID YOU KNOW?

New York City is sometimes called the "Big Apple," a term coined in the 1930s. Jazz musicians used the slang expression "apple" for any town or city. To play the Big Apple — New York City — was to play the big time.

New York City — the island of Manhattan in particular — is the cultural center of New York and a dominant cultural force throughout the world. It has everything from world-class museums to internationally renowned theater, as well as dance, classical music, jazz,

▼ **Times Square is the heart of Manhattan's theater district.**

rock-and-roll—the list goes on. Among the must-see sites in New York City is a fifteen-block stretch of Broadway known as The Great White Way, which includes famous 42nd Street. For over a hundred years, this has been New York's theater district, where dramas, comedies, and musicals are performed every night.

Acting runs in the blood of many New Yorkers. From the nineteenth century through the 1930s, New York was the center of the filmmaking industry. Radio then became an important industry in New York, and the television industry got its start here as well.

▲ Henry Cole, a painter in the Hudson River School, painted *Notch of the White Mountains* in 1839.

Music and dance are performed most nights. Lincoln Center is home to the New York City Ballet, the New York Philharmonic, and the Metropolitan Opera Company. Nearby Carnegie Hall hosts musical events of every kind.

While New York City is considered the cultural capital of New York and a major international culture and entertainment center, the rest of the state has a lot to offer. In 1825 the beauty of the Hudson River Valley inspired the first truly American genre of painting known as the Hudson River School. Artists such as Asher Durand and Thomas Cole, spurred by nationalistic pride and a love of untouched wilderness, believed that their paintings showed God's work in the beauty of nature.

Today the Hudson River is still alive with beauty, but nearly two hundred years of industrialization have taken their toll. In 1969 a massive cleanup effort was undertaken, spearheaded by folksinger Pete Seeger, skippering a tall ship with a 108-foot (33-m) mast and 5,000 square feet (465 sq m) of sail. The *Clearwater* teaches the importance of ecological conservation and the restoration of the Hudson River's environment. Every year, more than sixteen thousand school-age children get the chance to board the ship and learn how to help spread the message.

Also along the shores of the Hudson River is West Point. Founded in 1778, it is the oldest military academy and the oldest continuously operated military post in the nation. At

The Apollo Theater

Some of the best African-American musicians, dancers, and comedians have performed regularly at this landmark theater, in New York City's Harlem neighborhood. Many, including James Brown, Gladys Knight, and Sarah Vaughn, got their start at the theater's famous amateur night. Ironically, when the theater opened in 1914, it was restricted to whites only. Not until the 1930s was it open to everyone.

◀ The Guggenheim Museum in New York City was designed by Frank Lloyd Wright and opened in 1959.

Trophy Point, tourists can see the 500-yard (457-m) chain that stretched across the Hudson at West Point during the Revolutionary War as a barrier to enemy ships. Ulysses S. Grant, Robert E. Lee, Dwight Eisenhower, Douglas MacArthur, and George Patton all attended the school.

To the east of New York City lies Long Island, across which sprawls the boroughs of Queens and Brooklyn, as well as the suburbs of Nassau and Suffolk Counties. Along the Atlantic shore lie glistening white sand beaches.

On Long Island's northern shore is the Sagamore Hill National Historical Site, originally the summer home of Theodore Roosevelt. Today the house is a museum, furnished as it was when Roosevelt lived there.

North of New York City, in the Albany-Capital region, is historic Saratoga Springs. This longtime summer resort retreat has a racetrack that dates back to 1863. Today it is also home to the National Museum of Racing and Hall of Fame, a tribute to one of the United States' oldest sports. Saratoga is also home to the Saratoga Performing Arts Center, the summer home of the New York City Ballet, the New York City Opera, and the Philadelphia Orchestra.

West of Saratoga is New York's Central-Leatherstocking region. The region gets its name because it is central to the state and is also the area about which author James Fenimore Cooper wrote in his *Leatherstocking Tales*. This region is full of scenic beauty but of particular interest to baseball lovers, since Cooperstown is the home of the National Baseball Hall of Fame. It is also the hometown of James Fenimore Cooper. In addition to the baseball museum, this area also features a farm museum and a collection of buildings from the late 1700s and early 1800s.

Farther west, the Finger Lakes region attracts history buffs and tourists alike. The region's many lakes provide boating and fishing, while in Seneca Falls, there's the Women's Rights National Historical Park. Within the park boundaries are the home of suffragist Elizabeth Cady Stanton; Wesleyan Chapel, the site of the first women's rights convention; and the McClintock House, where Elizabeth Cady Stanton drafted the Declaration of Sentiments.

When it comes to tourist attractions, Niagara Falls, in the northwestern corner of the state, is tops not only in the state, but around the world. The 282-foot (86-m) tall Niagara Falls is often referred to as one of the seven wonders of the natural world. Located in Niagara Falls State Park, the oldest state park in the nation, the falls can be viewed from the tour boat *Maid of the Mist*. The famous falls are not the only attraction to visit in the Niagara area. At the Daredevil Museum you can learn about all the successful — and not so successful — people who have attempted to ride over Niagara Falls in a barrel.

◀ More than 6 million cubic feet (168,000 cubic m) of water go over Niagara Falls every second.

▲ Jackie Robinson.

Sports

New Yorkers love sports. In addition to legendary Yankee Stadium and Madison Square Garden, New York is home to many sports venues, including Shea Stadium and the USTA National Tennis Center. Tennis's annual final Grand Slam event, the U.S. Open, is played here in early September. Belmont Park, on Long Island, is home to the Belmont Stakes, one of horseracing's Triple Crown events.

DID YOU KNOW?

The Dodgers came into being as the "Bridegrooms." It was the team's move to the New York City borough of Brooklyn that led to the team's name "The Dodgers" — so-called because spectators had to "dodge" trolley cars to reach Ebbet's Field. The Dodgers were the first twentieth-century major league baseball team to integrate, when the legendary Jackie Robinson joined the squad in 1947.

Education

An important foundation to New York's commitment to the arts and culture in general is education. New York is a leader nationwide in providing affordable higher education, with a state university system consisting of sixty-four campuses throughout the state. New York City has its own university, the City University of New York (CUNY), which consists of eleven senior colleges, six community colleges, a graduate school, a law school, and a medical school.

Sport	Team	Home
Baseball	New York Yankees	Yankee Stadium, the Bronx
	New York Mets	Shea Stadium, Queens
Basketball	New York Knicks	Madison Square Garden, Manhattan
Women's Basketball	New York Liberty	Madison Square Garden, Manhattan
Football	New York Giants	Giants Stadium, East Rutherford, New Jersey
	New York Jets	Giants Stadium, East Rutherford, New Jersey
	Buffalo Bills	Ralph Wilson Stadium, Buffalo
Hockey	New York Islanders	Nassau Veterans Memorial Coliseum, Uniondale
	New York Rangers	Madison Square Garden, Manhattan
	Buffalo Sabers	HSBC Arena
Soccer	New York Power	Memorial Stadium, New Brunswick, New Jersey

In addition, the state is home to more than one hundred private colleges and universities. Among them are two Ivy League schools, Cornell University in Ithaca and Columbia University in Manhattan.

Baseball Firsts

▶ June 1851 — Two teams from different states compete. The New York Knicker-bockers play the Washington Base Ball Club at the Red House Grounds in New York.

▶ March 1858 — The first baseball game to charge admission is played between the Brooklyn All-Stars and the New York All-Stars.

▶ December 25, 1862 — Forty thousand Union troops watch a team from the 165th New York Volunteer Infantry play — probably the largest sporting event of the 1800s.

▶ March 1871 — The first professional baseball league is organized in New York City.

▶ 1920 — With Babe Ruth as leadoff hitter, the Yankees clinch the first of their thirty-three World Series. Other legendary Yankees include Joe DiMaggio, Mickey Mantle, Roger Maris, and Derek Jeter.

◀ The Brooklyn Dodgers of 1911. Many Brooklynites still mourn the Dodgers's move to Los Angeles in 1958.

Empire Builders

What does define "a New Yorker"? Not place of birth or accent of speech —
not in New York, famous for its welcome to newcomers of every geographic,
ethnic, and religious background.

— *Theodore C. Sorenson*

Following are only a few of the thousands of people who lived, died, or spent most of their
lives in New York and made extraordinary contributions to the state and the nation.

ALEXANDER HAMILTON
STATESMAN

BORN: *circa 1755, Nevis, British West Indies*
DIED: *July 12, 1804, New York City*

Alexander Hamilton
arrived in New York
in June of 1773 as a
prospective medical
student, most likely
intending to return
to his native West
Indies to open a
practice. Instead he
became one of the
United States' founding fathers.
Hamilton was a lieutenant colonel in
the Continental Army and served as
an aide to George Washington. Perhaps
most importantly, he, James Madison,
and John Jay penned The Federalist
Papers under the pseudonym "Publius."

WALT WHITMAN
POET

BORN: *May 31, 1819, West Hills*
DIED: *March 26, 1892, Camden, NJ*

Walt Whitman was a poet,
journalist, and essayist whose
verse collection *Leaves of
Grass* is a landmark in the
history of American
literature. He was inspired
to write poetry by his love
of nature, his experiences
during the Civil War, and
his sadness over the
assassination of Abraham
Lincoln. Throughout his
life, however, Whitman
continued to believe that
nature could restore the
soul, and his timeless
poetry reflects that.

KATE MULLANY
REFORMER

BORN: *circa 1845, Ireland*
DIED: *circa 1906, Troy*

Fourteen-hour workdays in sweltering heat. The pay? Two dollars a week. Irish immigrant Kate Mullany organized a union in protest of these conditions and, together with two hundred other female workers, successfully held a strike and gained a pay raise. Mullany was one of the labor movement's earliest female leaders. Although labor unions had been on the rise for decades, the union Mullany formed continued to exist for five years. (Most labor unions of the time lasted for only months.) In 1868 National Labor Union President William Sylvis appointed her to a labor union's national office, making her the first woman to hold such a position.

JACOB RIIS
PHOTOGRAPHER AND REFORMER

BORN: *May 3, 1849 Ribe, Denmark*
DIED: *May 26, 1914, Barre, MA*

Photographer and social reformer Jacob August Riis emigrated to the United States from Denmark. His job as a New York City police reporter meant he encountered the city's underbelly. Horrified by the poverty he encountered, he used his camera and the then-new flashbulbs to document the life in the Lower East Side's crowded tenement houses, where infant mortality ran as high as 90 percent. In 1890 he published his illustrations and photographs in his book *How the Other Half Lives*, shocking social reformers into action. Theodore Roosevelt himself told Riis, "I have read your book, and I have come to help."

▼ From Jacob Riis's book *How the Other Half Lives* — a New York City tenement apartment.

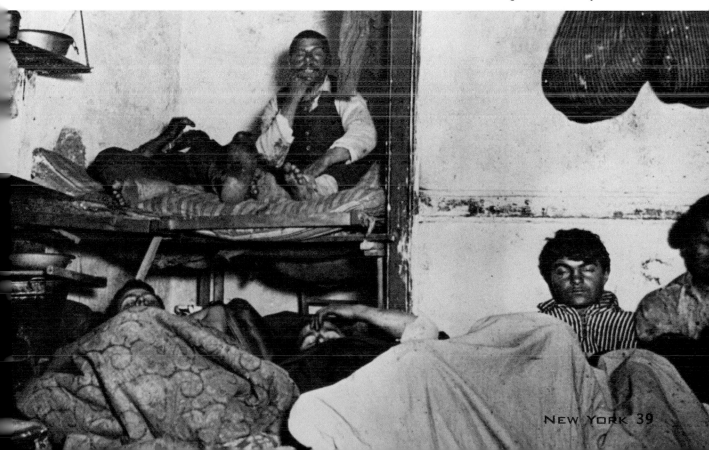

THEODORE ROOSEVELT
POLITICIAN AND STATESMAN

BORN: *October 27, 1858, New York City*
DIED: *January 6, 1918, Oyster Bay, NY*

Teddy Roosevelt's accomplishments are legendary; among them, he was the youngest person to assume the U.S. presidency. He was also the governor of New York, a deputy sheriff in the Dakota Territory, police commissioner of New York City, assistant secretary of the Navy, and colonel of the Rough Riders. Roosevelt became vice president in 1901 and assumed the presidency after William McKinley was shot. He also won a Nobel Peace Prize for negotiating the end to the Russo-Japanese War.

MATTHEW ALEXANDER HENSON
EXPLORER

BORN: *August 8, 1866, Charles County, MD*
DIED: *March 9, 1955, New York City*

Born in Maryland, African-American Matthew Henson went to sea at age twelve as a cabin boy. A chance meeting with explorer Robert E. Peary in 1888 led to Henson's career as an explorer and adventurer. On April 6, 1909, together with Perry and four Inuits, he became one of the first men known to have reached the North Pole. From 1929 until his death in 1955, Henson lived in the Dunbar apartments in New York City, where his apartment is now a national landmark.

FRANKLIN DELANO ROOSEVELT
POLITICIAN AND STATESMAN

BORN: *January 30, 1882, Hyde Park*
DIED: *April 12, 1945, Warm Springs, GA*

Franklin Roosevelt (FDR) is the only person elected to the presidency four times. During his years in office, he led the United States through two of the twentieth century's great crises — the Great Depression and World War II. Roosevelt is best known for his *Fireside Chats,* broadcast on the radio, and for his New Deal, which greatly expanded social programs in the United States. Although it was not publicly acknowledged at the time, Roosevelt had been stricken by polio and was, in fact, the United States' first physically disabled president.

LANGSTON HUGHES
POET

BORN: *February 1, 1902, Joplin, MO*
DIED: *May 22, 1967, New York City*

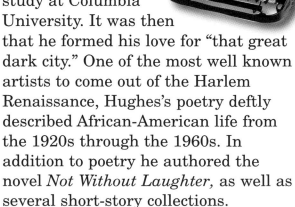

James Mercer Langston Hughes began his life in Joplin, Missouri, but came to Harlem to study at Columbia University. It was then that he formed his love for "that great dark city." One of the most well known artists to come out of the Harlem Renaissance, Hughes's poetry deftly described African-American life from the 1920s through the 1960s. In addition to poetry he authored the novel *Not Without Laughter,* as well as several short-story collections.

JACQUELINE KENNEDY ONASSIS
FIRST LADY, JOURNALIST, AND EDITOR

BORN: *July 28, 1929, Southampton*
DIED: *May 19, 1994, New York City*

Jacqueline Kennedy Onassis is best known as the wife of President John F. Kennedy, but prior to that, she was a journalist and photographer for the *Washington Times-Herald*. In 1951 she met John F. Kennedy when he was a congressman for the state of Massachusetts. They married in 1953. During her time as First Lady, she restored the White House and established the White House Historical Association. Immensely popular at home and abroad, her style was copied widely. After her husband's assassination in 1963, she returned to New York City and eventually remarried. Her marriage to Greek shipping magnate Aristotle Onassis lasted until his death in 1975. After his death she returned to publishing and worked as a book editor.

RUDY GIULIANI
POLITICIAN

BORN: *May 28, 1944, Brooklyn*

Rudolph Giuliani, grandson of Italian immigrants and graduate of New York University Law School, served as U.S. attorney for the Southern District of New York from 1983 to 1993. In this role he made a name for himself by leading efforts to stamp out organized crime. In 1993 he became the 107th mayor of New York City. During Giuliani's eight years in office, New York was named the safest large city in the United States five times by the FBI. Due to term limits, Giuliani's second term would be his last. While undergoing treatment for prostate cancer, Giuliani presided over the city during the worst crisis in its history, the destruction by terrorists of the World Trade Center in September 2001. Even though there was considerable public support for an extension of his final term, or for the repeal of term limits so that he could run for a third, any such attempts to keep Giuliani in office were deemed unconstitutional.

KEITH HARING
ARTIST

BORN: *May 4, 1958, Reading, PA*
DIED: *February 16, 1990, New York City*

In 1978 at the age of twenty, Keith Haring moved to New York City and enrolled at the School of Visual Arts. Haring was inspired by graffiti art on the subways and walls around New York City and began creating his own chalk works in the graffiti style. The drawings were of flying saucers, human figures, television sets, animals, and babies. He then translated his art style to canvas with bold, brightly colored works. Eventually, Haring was invited to exhibit all over the world. He used his art to bring attention to critical problems — illiteracy, drug use, and AIDS awareness— as well as calls to support UNICEF and the anti-apartheid movement. Haring died from AIDS-related causes at the age of thirty-one.

New York

History At-A-Glance

1524
Giovanni da Verrazzano becomes the first European to see New York.

1609
Englishman Henry Hudson claims area at the mouth of what is now the Hudson River for the Dutch and calls it New Netherlands.

1609
Frenchman Samuel de Champlain sails down the Hudson, staking a French claim to the territory.

1624
Dutch settle Fort Orange on the site of present-day Albany.

1625
The Dutch settle New Amsterdam on the site of present-day New York City.

1664
New Amsterdam is conquered by the English and renamed New York after the Duke of York in 1669.

1776
New York signs the Declaration of Independence, one of the thirteen original colonies that broke from England.

1777
Battle of Saratoga, turning point of Revolutionary War, is won by colonies.

1788
New York adopts a state constitution and becomes a state, July 26.

1789
George Washington is inaugurated first president of the United States in New York City.

1792
Founding of New York Stock Exchange establishes New York as financial center of the country.

1799
First steps toward abolition of slavery in New York.

1600   **1700**   **1800**

1492
Christopher Columbus comes to the New World.

1607
Capt. John Smith and three ships land on Virginia coast and start first English settlement in New World — Jamestown.

1754–63
French and Indian War.

1773
Boston Tea Party.

1776
Declaration of Independence adopted July 4.

1777
Articles of Confederation adopted by Continental Congress.

1787
U.S. Constitution written.

1812–14
War of 1812.

United States

History At-A-Glance

▼ **Downtown Manhattan as seen from Brooklyn in 1913.**

1809
Robert Fulton's *Clermont* makes a trip up the Hudson, the first successful voyage of a steamboat, with an operating speed of 5 mph (8 km/h).

1825
Erie Canal completed, linking the Hudson River with the Great Lakes and ushering in a prosperous new era of shipping and commerce.

1831
New York's first railroad, the Mohawk and Hudson, begins running between Albany and Schenectady.

1848
The Seneca Falls Convention paves the way for women's rights.

1863
Civil War anti-draft riots in New York City result in thousands of deaths and millions of dollars worth of damage.

1883
The Brooklyn Bridge is completed, connecting Manhattan with Brooklyn.

1886
Statue of Liberty dedicated on October 28 by President Grover Cleveland.

1907
Peak immigration year: 1.3 million people pass through Ellis Island, which opened in 1898.

1911
Triangle Shirtwaist fire kills 146 women workers, leading to reforms.

1946
New York becomes the permanent headquarters of the United Nations.

1959
St. Lawrence Seaway opens.

2000
Hillary Clinton is elected U.S. senator from New York, the first First Lady in the Senate.

2001
Terrorists hijack two airliners and crash into New York City's World Trade Center, leaving thousands dead or injured. Rescue and recovery workers labor tirelessly at the site, earning the city's gratitude.

1800   **1900**   **2000**

1848
Gold discovered in California draws 80,000 prospectors in the 1849 Gold Rush.

1861–65
Civil War.

1869
Transcontinental railroad is completed.

1917–18
U.S. involvement in World War I.

1929
Stock market crash ushers in Great Depression.

1941–45
U.S. involvement in World War II.

1950–53
U.S. fights in the Korean War.

1964–73
U.S. involvement in Vietnam War.

2000
George W. Bush wins the closest presidential election in history.

2001
A terrorist attack in which four hijacked airliners crash into New York City's World Trade Center, the Pentagon, and farmland in western Pennsylvania leaves thousands dead or injured.

Festivals and Fun For All

Check web site for exact date and directions.

Adirondack Balloon Festival, Lake George

As the fall foliage emerges and the leaves turn brilliant colors, the sky is filled with brilliant balloons during this annual festival. A great reason to visit the Adirondack region.

www.adirondackballoonfestival.com

Adirondack Theatre Festival, Glens Falls

During each four-week summer season, the festival produces at least three plays, from Broadway shows to world premieres. There are also workshops, readings, and discussions.

www.ATFestival.org

▼ Walkers on the Brooklyn Bridge.

Chenango Blues Festival, Norwich

One of the larger blues festivals outside of New York City features great music, food, and area attractions.

www.blackdogweb.com/bluesfest

Hudson Valley Shakespeare Festival, Cold Spring

The Hudson Valley Shakespeare Festival is an annual celebration of the plays of William Shakespeare.

hvshakespeare.org

LaFayette Apple Festival, LaFayette

Fall is the perfect foil for a festival celebrating New York apples. Tour scenic LaFayette and join in the apple-centered fun.

www.lafayetteapplefest.org

Lilac Festival, Rochester

Each May, the Lilac Festival commemorates the beginning of spring in historic Highland Park, as one-thousand and two hundred lilac bushes of more than five-hundred varieties bloom.

www.history.rochester.edu/class/sethfox/geninf.htm

► Lilacs bloom for Rochester's Lilac Festival.

New York State Fair, Syracuse

More than 200 acres (81 ha) of animals, exhibits, and displays, as well as live performances, midway rides, and games of skill. Nearly one million people visit every year.

www.nysfair.org

Seneca Lake Whale Watch, Geneva

Arts and crafts, great food, and three days of whale watching make a great adventure for the whole family.

www.senecalakewhalewatch.com

Syracuse Nationals, Syracuse

Classic car enthusiasts gather together at the "Largest Car Happening On The East Coast" for food and fun.

www.syracusenats.com

Tomato Fest, Owasco Lake Auburn

A celebration of tomatoes and a fundraiser for area food agencies. Music and folk art round out this family-centered event.

cayuganet.org/tomatofest

▲ Balloons rise during the Adirondack Balloon Festival.

New York City Parades and Street Celebrations

Every year, hundreds of parades are held throughout the city, reflecting the city's diverse ethnic heritage. Here are just a few:

January

New Year's Eve: Millions join together in Times Square to watch the ball drop at midnight.

February

Chinese New Year: Dragons, dancers, and drums create a different sort of New Year's celebration. Held in Manhattan's Chinatown.

March

St. Patrick's Day Parade: The first St. Patrick's Day Parade was held in 1766 — the first in the Americas. The parade follows Fifth Avenue from 44th to 86th Street, in Manhattan.

June

The Puerto Rican Day Parade: The first Puerto Rican Day Parade was held in New York in 1958.

The parade follows Fifth Avenue from 44th to 86th Street in Manhattan.

July

Macy's Fireworks Display: A gigantic fireworks display held on the East River between Brooklyn and Manhattan.

November

The New York City Marathon: A 26.2-mile (42-km) marathon that traverses New York City's five boroughs, starting in Staten Island, and finishing in Manhattan's Central Park.

Macy's Thanksgiving Day Parade: An annual parade held every year since 1924 and nationally televised since 1948.

Books

Chambers, Veronica, Josh Wilker, and B. Marvis. *The Harlem Renaissance*. New York: Chelsea House Publishing, 1997. Learn more about this exciting time in American culture and African-American history.

Doherty, Craig A., Katherine M. Doherty, and Nicole Bowman. *The Erie Canal*. Woodbridge, CT: Blackbirch Marketing, 1996. Find out more about this important waterway, which was the highway of a former era.

Fradin, Dennis Brindel. *The New York Colony*. Danbury, CT: Children's Press, 1998. Learn about the history of Dutch and English settlement in New York State.

Hansen, Joyce, and Gary McGowan. *Breaking Ground, Breaking Silence: The Story of New York's African Burial Ground*. New York: Henry Holt & Co., Inc, 1998. The discovery of a colonial-era graveyard sheds light on New York City's history.

Kalman, Bobbie, and Lewis Parker. *Life in a Longhouse Village*. New York: Crabtree Pub., 2001. Life in New York State before European settlers arrived.

Web Sites

▶ Official state web site
www.iloveny.state.ny.us

▶ Official Albany web site
www.albanyny.org

▶ Official New York City web site
www.nyc.gov

▶ A guide to historical markers throughout New York State
www.nysm.nysed.gov/srv/largemarkers/inventoryone.html

▶ Long Island history site
www.lihistory.com

▶ New York State Newspaper Project: Signifigant newspapers published in New York since 1725
www.nysl.nysed.gov/nysnp

Films

Burns, Ric. *New York: A Documentary Film*. Boston: Steeplechase Films/WGBH, 2000. An excellent and informative documentary film about New York State.

INDEX

Note: Page numbers in *italics* refer to illustrations or photographs.